Words
of the
Angel Circle

Words
of the
Angel Circle

And Journal of Gratitude

Lorianne Nunes

BALBOA
PRESS

A DIVISION OF HAY HOUSE

Balboa Press books may be ordered through booksellers or by contacting:

Balboa Press
A Division of Hay House
1663 Liberty Drive
Bloomington, IN 47403
www.balboapress.com
1-(877) 407-4847

Because of the dynamic nature of the Internet, any web addresses or links contained in this book may have changed since publication and may no longer be valid. The views expressed in this work are solely those of the author and do not necessarily reflect the views of the publisher, and the publisher hereby disclaims any responsibility for them.

The author of this book does not dispense medical advice or prescribe the use of any technique as a form of treatment for physical, emotional, or medical problems without the advice of a physician, either directly or indirectly. The intent of the author is only to offer information of a general nature to help you in your quest for emotional and spiritual well-being. In the event you use any of the information in this book for yourself, which is your constitutional right, the author and the publisher assume no responsibility for your actions.

Any people depicted in stock imagery provided by Thinkstock are models, and such images are being used for illustrative purposes only.
Certain stock imagery © Thinkstock.

ISBN: 978-1-4525-3492-3 (e)
ISBN: 978-1-4525-3491-6 (sc)

Printed in the United States of America

Balboa Press rev. date: 5/24/2011

To God & the Angels you are my light my breath my soul…

To my two beautiful daughters Karissa and Candice, you
both have taught me that I can accomplish anything.
To my Husband Christopher, my best friend, who has always encouraged me
to follow my dreams, You are my light at the end of the tunnel I Love you.
To All my friends, Karen, Heaven on Earth you lead me to the path
where my journey began, Christine & Dora my Sisters of Solace
You gave me a place to practice & grow. To my Angel Circle family
thank you for being you. And to Dotti of Positive New Beginnings
you truly believed in me and for that I am forever grateful.
My Family& friends
I Love you all
Angel Blessings
Lorianne

I decided to put this journal together for my Angels circle group, this is a group that I hold once a week. It's an open forum. We start the class by everyone picking an "Angel Oracle Card" and we go around the circle for everyone to share what their card is and how they feel it fits into their life. We hold discussions on how to handle different everyday situations using Love & not fear. The people in this circle have truly become like family to each other. In one of the angel circles I had read a passage from an angel guidance book and gave them all a note card to write what they felt the message was in that passage, on the outside of the note cards were butterflies and 3 words Hope, Believe, and Faith. Just as the circle was closing the angels guided me to have them take the three words on the card and sometime before the next circle to sit quietly and meditate on one word at a time and ask their angels for guidance using that word as a starting point. Over the course of a couple of days I started posting a "word of the day" on My Angel Circle group on Facebook it became very popular. One day I forgot to post a word and I started getting messages on Facebook asking where the word was, they really looked forward to that simple little word. At that moment I realized that so many others could benefit from my "Word of the day." I was compelled to share. Even though it was originally created for my Angel circle family, I do believe that anyone can benefit from its use.

I hope you enjoy this experience as much as they have.

The "Word of the day"

This Journal book is for anyone that wants to make a positive change in their lives. Anyone can enjoy and benefit from the use of this book at anytime of the day, whether it be to start each day on a positive note, a mid day break from the craziness of everyday life, or as a night time meditation/relaxation before you close your eyes to go to sleep. You can go in order from beginning to end, you can randomly pick a page, or you can look through the pages to see which word resonates with you for that day, there is no right or wrong way. You choose what works best, this is all about you!

To begin:

Get comfortable, whether it be sitting in a chair or lying on a bed, where ever you feel relaxed. Take a deep breath in through your nose and out through your mouth. Let your breathing relax your mind and your body. Now think of your Word. How does that word make you feel? What comes to mind when you think of this word? How does this word fit into your life now? How would you like this word to fit into your life in the future? What are your thoughts? Then sit quietly and begin to journal your thoughts….

The Gratitude Journal

How often have you sat quietly and thought about all the things in your life that you have to be thankful for? We all tend to get wrapped up in our everyday busy lives that we sometimes forget all that we do have to be thankful for. To remind us I have suggested my clients to create a Gratitude Journal it is a way to remind us that we have so much to be grateful for and when we show gratitude to the universe we open ourselves up to receive even more.
What I suggest is every night before you go to sleep write down 10 things that you are grateful for in your life. It can be something as simple as getting the perfect cup of coffee that morning, or maybe being grateful for the perfect parking space you were able to get at the grocery store it's that simple. By doing this you will be able to look back any time you need a reminder of how truly blessed you are.

I am truly grateful for being able to share my book with everyone. Blessings…

The Word of the Day is:

Believe

Sit quietly and relax. Now take a deep breath in through your nose and exhale slowly through your mouth. Take time to meditate on this word. What does the word mean to you? What messages do the Angels have for you regarding this word? What comes to mind? Now write it down.

Today's Date: _____

Gratitude Journal

Take a minute to think of all the things that life has given you to be thankful for.
Now I'd like you to write down ten things that you are grateful for…

1 _____
2 _____
3 _____
4 _____
5 _____
6 _____
7 _____
8 _____
9 _____
10 _____

Thank you for these wonderful blessings in my life.

Other thoughts of the day

_____
_____
_____
_____
_____
_____
_____
_____
_____
_____
_____
_____
_____
_____
_____
_____

The Word of the Day is:

Gratitude

Sit quietly and relax. Now take a deep breath in through your nose and exhale slowly through your mouth. Take time to meditate on this word. What does the word mean to you? What messages do the Angels have for you regarding this word? What comes to mind? Now write it down.

Today's Date: _____

Gratitude Journal

Take a minute to think of all the things that life has given you to be thankful for.
Now I'd like you to write down ten things that you are grateful for…

1 _____
2 _____
3 _____
4 _____
5 _____
6 _____
7 _____
8 _____
9 _____
10 _____

Thank you for these wonderful blessings in my life.

Other thoughts of the day

_____
_____
_____
_____
_____
_____
_____
_____
_____
_____
_____
_____
_____
_____
_____
_____
_____

The Word of the Day is:

Reflect

Sit quietly and relax. Now take a deep breath in through your nose and exhale slowly through your mouth. Take time to meditate on this word. What does the word mean to you? What messages do the Angels have for you regarding this word? What comes to mind? Now write it down.

Today's Date: _____

Gratitude Journal

Take a minute to think of all the things that life has given you to be thankful for. Now I'd like you to write down ten things that you are grateful for...

1 _____
2 _____
3 _____
4 _____
5 _____
6 _____
7 _____
8 _____
9 _____
10 _____

Thank you for these wonderful blessings in my life.

Other thoughts of the day

_____
_____
_____
_____
_____
_____
_____
_____
_____
_____
_____
_____
_____
_____
_____
_____

The Word of the Day is:

Compassion

Sit quietly and relax. Now take a deep breath in through your nose and exhale slowly through your mouth. Take time to meditate on this word. What does the word mean to you? What messages do the Angels have for you regarding this word? What comes to mind? Now write it down.

Today's Date: _____

Gratitude Journal

Take a minute to think of all the things that life has given you to be thankful for.
Now I'd like you to write down ten things that you are grateful for...

1 _____
2 _____
3 _____
4 _____
5 _____
6 _____
7 _____
8 _____
9 _____
10 _____

Thank you for these wonderful blessings in my life.

Other thoughts of the day

_____
_____
_____
_____
_____
_____
_____
_____
_____
_____
_____
_____
_____
_____
_____
_____
_____

The Word of the Day is:

Grace

Sit quietly and relax. Now take a deep breath in through your nose and exhale slowly through your mouth. Take time to meditate on this word. What does the word mean to you? What messages do the Angels have for you regarding this word? What comes to mind? Now write it down.

Today's Date: _____

Gratitude Journal

Take a minute to think of all the things that life has given you to be thankful for.
Now I'd like you to write down ten things that you are grateful for...

1 _____
2 _____
3 _____
4 _____
5 _____
6 _____
7 _____
8 _____
9 _____
10 _____

Thank you for these wonderful blessings in my life.

Other thoughts of the day

_____
_____
_____
_____
_____
_____
_____
_____
_____
_____
_____
_____
_____
_____
_____
_____

The Word of the Day is:

Faith

Sit quietly and relax. Now take a deep breath in through your nose and exhale slowly through your mouth. Take time to meditate on this word. What does the word mean to you? What messages do the Angels have for you regarding this word? What comes to mind? Now write it down.

Today's Date: _____

Gratitude Journal

Take a minute to think of all the things that life has given you to be thankful for.
Now I'd like you to write down ten things that you are grateful for...

1 _____
2 _____
3 _____
4 _____
5 _____
6 _____
7 _____
8 _____
9 _____
10 _____

Thank you for these wonderful blessings in my life.

Other thoughts of the day

_____
_____
_____
_____
_____
_____
_____
_____
_____
_____
_____
_____
_____
_____
_____
_____
_____
_____

The Word of the Day is:

Forgiveness

Sit quietly and relax. Now take a deep breath in through your nose and exhale slowly through your mouth. Take time to meditate on this word. What does the word mean to you? What messages do the Angels have for you regarding this word? What comes to mind? Now write it down.

Today's Date: _____

Gratitude Journal

Take a minute to think of all the things that life has given you to be thankful for.
Now I'd like you to write down ten things that you are grateful for...

1 _____
2 _____
3 _____
4 _____
5 _____
6 _____
7 _____
8 _____
9 _____
10 _____

Thank you for these wonderful blessings in my life.

Other thoughts of the day

_____
_____
_____
_____
_____
_____
_____
_____
_____
_____
_____
_____
_____
_____
_____
_____

The Word of the Day is:

Joy

Sit quietly and relax. Now take a deep breath in through your nose and exhale slowly through your mouth. Take time to meditate on this word. What does the word mean to you? What messages do the Angels have for you regarding this word? What comes to mind? Now write it down.

Today's Date: _____

Gratitude Journal

Take a minute to think of all the things that life has given you to be thankful for.
Now I'd like you to write down ten things that you are grateful for...

1 _____
2 _____
3 _____
4 _____
5 _____
6 _____
7 _____
8 _____
9 _____
10 _____

Thank you for these wonderful blessings in my life.

Other thoughts of the day

_____
_____
_____
_____
_____
_____
_____
_____
_____
_____
_____
_____
_____
_____
_____
_____

The Word of the Day is:

Cherish

Sit quietly and relax. Now take a deep breath in through your nose and exhale slowly through your mouth. Take time to meditate on this word. What does the word mean to you? What messages do the Angels have for you regarding this word? What comes to mind? Now write it down.

Today's Date: _____

Gratitude Journal

Take a minute to think of all the things that life has given you to be thankful for.
Now I'd like you to write down ten things that you are grateful for...

1 _____
2 _____
3 _____
4 _____
5 _____
6 _____
7 _____
8 _____
9 _____
10 _____

Thank you for these wonderful blessings in my life.

Other thoughts of the day

_____
_____
_____
_____
_____
_____
_____
_____
_____
_____
_____
_____
_____
_____
_____
_____

The Word of the Day is:

Rejoice

Sit quietly and relax. Now take a deep breath in through your nose and exhale slowly through your mouth. Take time to meditate on this word. What does the word mean to you? What messages do the Angels have for you regarding this word? What comes to mind? Now write it down.

Today's Date: _____

Gratitude Journal

Take a minute to think of all the things that life has given you to be thankful for.
Now I'd like you to write down ten things that you are grateful for...

1 _____
2 _____
3 _____
4 _____
5 _____
6 _____
7 _____
8 _____
9 _____
10 _____

Thank you for these wonderful blessings in my life.

Other thoughts of the day

_____
_____
_____
_____
_____
_____
_____
_____
_____
_____
_____
_____
_____
_____
_____
_____

The Word of the Day is:

Hope

Sit quietly and relax. Now take a deep breath in through your nose and exhale slowly through your mouth. Take time to meditate on this word. What does the word mean to you? What messages do the Angels have for you regarding this word? What comes to mind? Now write it down.

Today's Date: _____

Gratitude Journal

Take a minute to think of all the things that life has given you to be thankful for.
Now I'd like you to write down ten things that you are grateful for…

1 _____
2 _____
3 _____
4 _____
5 _____
6 _____
7 _____
8 _____
9 _____
10 _____

Thank you for these wonderful blessings in my life.

Other thoughts of the day

_____
_____
_____
_____
_____
_____
_____
_____
_____
_____
_____
_____
_____
_____
_____
_____

The Word of the Day is:

Breath

Sit quietly and relax. Now take a deep breath in through your nose and exhale slowly through your mouth. Take time to meditate on this word. What does the word mean to you? What messages do the Angels have for you regarding this word? What comes to mind? Now write it down.

Today's Date: _____

Gratitude Journal

Take a minute to think of all the things that life has given you to be thankful for.
Now I'd like you to write down ten things that you are grateful for...

1 _____
2 _____
3 _____
4 _____
5 _____
6 _____
7 _____
8 _____
9 _____
10 _____

Thank you for these wonderful blessings in my life.

Other thoughts of the day

_____
_____
_____
_____
_____
_____
_____
_____
_____
_____
_____
_____
_____
_____

The Word of the Day is:

Trust

Sit quietly and relax. Now take a deep breath in through your nose and exhale slowly through your mouth. Take time to meditate on this word. What does the word mean to you? What messages do the Angels have for you regarding this word? What comes to mind? Now write it down.

Today's Date: _____

Gratitude Journal

Take a minute to think of all the things that life has given you to be thankful for.
Now I'd like you to write down ten things that you are grateful for…

1 _____
2 _____
3 _____
4 _____
5 _____
6 _____
7 _____
8 _____
9 _____
10 _____

Thank you for these wonderful blessings in my life.

Other thoughts of the day

_____
_____
_____
_____
_____
_____
_____
_____
_____
_____
_____
_____
_____
_____
_____
_____

The Word of the Day is:

Release

Sit quietly and relax. Now take a deep breath in through your nose and exhale slowly through your mouth. Take time to meditate on this word. What does the word mean to you? What messages do the Angels have for you regarding this word? What comes to mind? Now write it down.

Today's Date: _____

Gratitude Journal

Take a minute to think of all the things that life has given you to be thankful for.
Now I'd like you to write down ten things that you are grateful for...

1 _____
2 _____
3 _____
4 _____
5 _____
6 _____
7 _____
8 _____
9 _____
10 _____

Thank you for these wonderful blessings in my life.

Other thoughts of the day

_____
_____
_____
_____
_____
_____
_____
_____
_____
_____
_____
_____
_____
_____
_____
_____

The Word of the Day is:

Sit quietly and relax. Now take a deep breath in through your nose and exhale slowly through your mouth. Take time to meditate on this word. What does the word mean to you? What messages do the Angels have for you regarding this word? What comes to mind? Now write it down.

Today's Date: _____

Gratitude Journal

Take a minute to think of all the things that life has given you to be thankful for.
Now I'd like you to write down ten things that you are grateful for...

1 _____
2 _____
3 _____
4 _____
5 _____
6 _____
7 _____
8 _____
9 _____
10 _____

Thank you for these wonderful blessings in my life.

Other thoughts of the day

_____
_____
_____
_____
_____
_____
_____
_____
_____
_____
_____
_____
_____
_____
_____
_____
_____

The Word of the Day is:

Boundaries

Sit quietly and relax. Now take a deep breath in through your nose and exhale slowly through your mouth. Take time to meditate on this word. What does the word mean to you? What messages do the Angels have for you regarding this word? What comes to mind? Now write it down.

Today's Date: _____

Gratitude Journal

Take a minute to think of all the things that life has given you to be thankful for.
Now I'd like you to write down ten things that you are grateful for...

1 _____
2 _____
3 _____
4 _____
5 _____
6 _____
7 _____
8 _____
9 _____
10 _____

Thank you for these wonderful blessings in my life.

Other thoughts of the day

_____
_____
_____
_____
_____
_____
_____
_____
_____
_____
_____
_____
_____
_____
_____
_____

The Word of the Day is:

Intentions

Sit quietly and relax. Now take a deep breath in through your nose and exhale slowly through your mouth. Take time to meditate on this word. What does the word mean to you? What messages do the Angels have for you regarding this word? What comes to mind? Now write it down.

Today's Date: _____

Gratitude Journal

Take a minute to think of all the things that life has given you to be thankful for.
Now I'd like you to write down ten things that you are grateful for…

1 _____
2 _____
3 _____
4 _____
5 _____
6 _____
7 _____
8 _____
9 _____
10 _____

Thank you for these wonderful blessings in my life.

Other thoughts of the day

_____
_____
_____
_____
_____
_____
_____
_____
_____
_____
_____
_____
_____
_____
_____
_____

The Word of the Day is:

Dream

Sit quietly and relax. Now take a deep breath in through your nose and exhale slowly through your mouth. Take time to meditate on this word. What does the word mean to you? What messages do the Angels have for you regarding this word? What comes to mind? Now write it down.

Gratitude Journal

Take a minute to think of all the things that life has given you to be thankful for.
Now I'd like you to write down ten things that you are grateful for...

1 _____
2 _____
3 _____
4 _____
5 _____
6 _____
7 _____
8 _____
9 _____
10 _____

Thank you for these wonderful blessings in my life.

Other thoughts of the day

_____
_____
_____
_____
_____
_____
_____
_____
_____
_____
_____
_____
_____
_____
_____
_____
_____
_____

The Word of the Day is:

Listen

Sit quietly and relax. Now take a deep breath in through your nose and exhale slowly through your mouth. Take time to meditate on this word. What does the word mean to you? What messages do the Angels have for you regarding this word? What comes to mind? Now write it down.

Today's Date: _____

Gratitude Journal

Take a minute to think of all the things that life has given you to be thankful for.
Now I'd like you to write down ten things that you are grateful for…

1 _____
2 _____
3 _____
4 _____
5 _____
6 _____
7 _____
8 _____
9 _____
10 _____

Thank you for these wonderful blessings in my life.

Other thoughts of the day

_____
_____
_____
_____
_____
_____
_____
_____
_____
_____
_____
_____
_____
_____
_____
_____

The Word of the Day is:

Pray

Sit quietly and relax. Now take a deep breath in through your nose and exhale slowly through your mouth. Take time to meditate on this word. What does the word mean to you? What messages do the Angels have for you regarding this word? What comes to mind? Now write it down.

Today's Date: _____

Gratitude Journal

Take a minute to think of all the things that life has given you to be thankful for.
Now I'd like you to write down ten things that you are grateful for…

1 _____
2 _____
3 _____
4 _____
5 _____
6 _____
7 _____
8 _____
9 _____
10 _____

Thank you for these wonderful blessings in my life.

Other thoughts of the day

_____
_____
_____
_____
_____
_____
_____
_____
_____
_____
_____
_____
_____
_____
_____

The Word of the Day is:

Wisdom

Sit quietly and relax. Now take a deep breath in through your nose and exhale slowly through your mouth. Take time to meditate on this word. What does the word mean to you? What messages do the Angels have for you regarding this word? What comes to mind? Now write it down.

Today's Date: _____

Gratitude Journal

Take a minute to think of all the things that life has given you to be thankful for.
Now I'd like you to write down ten things that you are grateful for...

1 _____
2 _____
3 _____
4 _____
5 _____
6 _____
7 _____
8 _____
9 _____
10 _____

Thank you for these wonderful blessings in my life.

Other thoughts of the day

_____
_____
_____
_____
_____
_____
_____
_____
_____
_____
_____
_____
_____
_____
_____
_____

The Word of the Day is:

Guidance

Sit quietly and relax. Now take a deep breath in through your nose and exhale slowly through your mouth. Take time to meditate on this word. What does the word mean to you? What messages do the Angels have for you regarding this word? What comes to mind? Now write it down.

Today's Date: _____

Gratitude Journal

Take a minute to think of all the things that life has given you to be thankful for.
Now I'd like you to write down ten things that you are grateful for...

1 _____
2 _____
3 _____
4 _____
5 _____
6 _____
7 _____
8 _____
9 _____
10 _____

Thank you for these wonderful blessings in my life.

Other thoughts of the day

_____
_____
_____
_____
_____
_____
_____
_____
_____
_____
_____
_____
_____
_____
_____

The Word of the Day is:

Simplify

Sit quietly and relax. Now take a deep breath in through your nose and exhale slowly through your mouth. Take time to meditate on this word. What does the word mean to you? What messages do the Angels have for you regarding this word? What comes to mind? Now write it down.

Today's Date: _____

Gratitude Journal

Take a minute to think of all the things that life has given you to be thankful for.
Now I'd like you to write down ten things that you are grateful for...

1 _____
2 _____
3 _____
4 _____
5 _____
6 _____
7 _____
8 _____
9 _____
10 _____

Thank you for these wonderful blessings in my life.

Other thoughts of the day

_____
_____
_____
_____
_____
_____
_____
_____
_____
_____
_____
_____
_____
_____
_____
_____

The Word of the Day is:

Relax

Sit quietly and relax. Now take a deep breath in through your nose and exhale slowly through your mouth. Take time to meditate on this word. What does the word mean to you? What messages do the Angels have for you regarding this word? What comes to mind? Now write it down.

Today's Date: _____

Gratitude Journal

Take a minute to think of all the things that life has given you to be thankful for.
Now I'd like you to write down ten things that you are grateful for...

1 _____
2 _____
3 _____
4 _____
5 _____
6 _____
7 _____
8 _____
9 _____
10 _____

Thank you for these wonderful blessings in my life.

Other thoughts of the day

_____
_____
_____
_____
_____
_____
_____
_____
_____
_____
_____
_____
_____
_____
_____
_____
_____

The Word of the Day is:

Clarity

Sit quietly and relax. Now take a deep breath in through your nose and exhale slowly through your mouth. Take time to meditate on this word. What does the word mean to you? What messages do the Angels have for you regarding this word? What comes to mind? Now write it down.

Today's Date: _____

Gratitude Journal

Take a minute to think of all the things that life has given you to be thankful for.
Now I'd like you to write down ten things that you are grateful for...

1 _____
2 _____
3 _____
4 _____
5 _____
6 _____
7 _____
8 _____
9 _____
10 _____

Thank you for these wonderful blessings in my life.

Other thoughts of the day

_____
_____
_____
_____
_____
_____
_____
_____
_____
_____
_____
_____
_____
_____
_____
_____

The Word of the Day is:

Gentle

Sit quietly and relax. Now take a deep breath in through your nose and exhale slowly through your mouth. Take time to meditate on this word. What does the word mean to you? What messages do the Angels have for you regarding this word? What comes to mind? Now write it down.

Today's Date: _____

Gratitude Journal

Take a minute to think of all the things that life has given you to be thankful for.
Now I'd like you to write down ten things that you are grateful for…

1 _____
2 _____
3 _____
4 _____
5 _____
6 _____
7 _____
8 _____
9 _____
10 _____

Thank you for these wonderful blessings in my life.

Other thoughts of the day

_____
_____
_____
_____
_____
_____
_____
_____
_____
_____
_____
_____
_____
_____
_____
_____

The Word of the Day is:

Receive

Sit quietly and relax. Now take a deep breath in through your nose and exhale slowly through your mouth. Take time to meditate on this word. What does the word mean to you? What messages do the Angels have for you regarding this word? What comes to mind? Now write it down.

Today's Date: _____

Gratitude Journal

Take a minute to think of all the things that life has given you to be thankful for.
Now I'd like you to write down ten things that you are grateful for...

1 _____
2 _____
3 _____
4 _____
5 _____
6 _____
7 _____
8 _____
9 _____
10 _____

Thank you for these wonderful blessings in my life.

Other thoughts of the day

_____
_____
_____
_____
_____
_____
_____
_____
_____
_____
_____
_____
_____
_____
_____
_____
_____

The Word of the Day is:

Serenity

Sit quietly and relax. Now take a deep breath in through your nose and exhale slowly through your mouth. Take time to meditate on this word. What does the word mean to you? What messages do the Angels have for you regarding this word? What comes to mind? Now write it down.

Today's Date: _____

Gratitude Journal

Take a minute to think of all the things that life has given you to be thankful for.
Now I'd like you to write down ten things that you are grateful for...

1 _____
2 _____
3 _____
4 _____
5 _____
6 _____
7 _____
8 _____
9 _____
10 _____

Thank you for these wonderful blessings in my life.

Other thoughts of the day

_____
_____
_____
_____
_____
_____
_____
_____
_____
_____
_____
_____
_____
_____
_____

The Word of the Day is:

Passion

Sit quietly and relax. Now take a deep breath in through your nose and exhale slowly through your mouth. Take time to meditate on this word. What does the word mean to you? What messages do the Angels have for you regarding this word? What comes to mind? Now write it down.

Today's Date: _____

Gratitude Journal

Take a minute to think of all the things that life has given you to be thankful for.
Now I'd like you to write down ten things that you are grateful for...

1 _____
2 _____
3 _____
4 _____
5 _____
6 _____
7 _____
8 _____
9 _____
10 _____

Thank you for these wonderful blessings in my life.

Other thoughts of the day

_____
_____
_____
_____
_____
_____
_____
_____
_____
_____
_____
_____
_____
_____
_____
_____

The Word of the Day is:

Grateful

Sit quietly and relax. Now take a deep breath in through your nose and exhale slowly through your mouth. Take time to meditate on this word. What does the word mean to you? What messages do the Angels have for you regarding this word? What comes to mind? Now write it down.

Today's Date: _____

Gratitude Journal

Take a minute to think of all the things that life has given you to be thankful for.
Now I'd like you to write down ten things that you are grateful for...

1 _____
2 _____
3 _____
4 _____
5 _____
6 _____
7 _____
8 _____
9 _____
10 _____

Thank you for these wonderful blessings in my life.

Other thoughts of the day

_____
_____
_____
_____
_____
_____
_____
_____
_____
_____
_____
_____
_____
_____
_____
_____
_____

The Word of the Day is:

Lesson

Sit quietly and relax. Now take a deep breath in through your nose and exhale slowly through your mouth. Take time to meditate on this word. What does the word mean to you? What messages do the Angels have for you regarding this word? What comes to mind? Now write it down.

Today's Date: _____

Gratitude Journal

Take a minute to think of all the things that life has given you to be thankful for.
Now I'd like you to write down ten things that you are grateful for…

1 _____
2 _____
3 _____
4 _____
5 _____
6 _____
7 _____
8 _____
9 _____
10 _____

Thank you for these wonderful blessings in my life.

Other thoughts of the day

_____
_____
_____
_____
_____
_____
_____
_____
_____
_____
_____
_____
_____
_____
_____
_____

The Word of the Day is:

Create

Sit quietly and relax. Now take a deep breath in through your nose and exhale slowly through your mouth. Take time to meditate on this word. What does the word mean to you? What messages do the Angels have for you regarding this word? What comes to mind? Now write it down.

Today's Date: _____

Gratitude Journal

Take a minute to think of all the things that life has given you to be thankful for.
Now I'd like you to write down ten things that you are grateful for...

1 _____
2 _____
3 _____
4 _____
5 _____
6 _____
7 _____
8 _____
9 _____
10 _____

Thank you for these wonderful blessings in my life.

Other thoughts of the day

_____
_____
_____
_____
_____
_____
_____
_____
_____
_____
_____
_____
_____
_____
_____
_____

The Word of the Day is:

Nature

Sit quietly and relax. Now take a deep breath in through your nose and exhale slowly through your mouth. Take time to meditate on this word. What does the word mean to you? What messages do the Angels have for you regarding this word? What comes to mind? Now write it down.

Today's Date: _____

Gratitude Journal

Take a minute to think of all the things that life has given you to be thankful for. Now I'd like you to write down ten things that you are grateful for…

1 _____
2 _____
3 _____
4 _____
5 _____
6 _____
7 _____
8 _____
9 _____
10 _____

Thank you for these wonderful blessings in my life.

Other thoughts of the day

_____
_____
_____
_____
_____
_____
_____
_____
_____
_____
_____
_____
_____
_____
_____

The Word of the Day is:

Family

Sit quietly and relax. Now take a deep breath in through your nose and exhale slowly through your mouth. Take time to meditate on this word. What does the word mean to you? What messages do the Angels have for you regarding this word? What comes to mind? Now write it down.

Today's Date: _____

Gratitude Journal

Take a minute to think of all the things that life has given you to be thankful for.
Now I'd like you to write down ten things that you are grateful for...

1 _____
2 _____
3 _____
4 _____
5 _____
6 _____
7 _____
8 _____
9 _____
10 _____

Thank you for these wonderful blessings in my life.

Other thoughts of the day

_____
_____
_____
_____
_____
_____
_____
_____
_____
_____
_____
_____
_____
_____
_____

The Word of the Day is:

Communicate

Sit quietly and relax. Now take a deep breath in through your nose and exhale slowly through your mouth. Take time to meditate on this word. What does the word mean to you? What messages do the Angels have for you regarding this word? What comes to mind? Now write it down.

Today's Date: _____

Gratitude Journal

Take a minute to think of all the things that life has given you to be thankful for.
Now I'd like you to write down ten things that you are grateful for...

1 _____
2 _____
3 _____
4 _____
5 _____
6 _____
7 _____
8 _____
9 _____
10 _____

Thank you for these wonderful blessings in my life.

Other thoughts of the day

_____
_____
_____
_____
_____
_____
_____
_____
_____
_____
_____
_____
_____
_____
_____
_____

The Word of the Day is:

Bliss

Sit quietly and relax. Now take a deep breath in through your nose and exhale slowly through your mouth. Take time to meditate on this word. What does the word mean to you? What messages do the Angels have for you regarding this word? What comes to mind? Now write it down.

Today's Date: _____

Gratitude Journal

Take a minute to think of all the things that life has given you to be thankful for.
Now I'd like you to write down ten things that you are grateful for...

1 _____
2 _____
3 _____
4 _____
5 _____
6 _____
7 _____
8 _____
9 _____
10 _____

Thank you for these wonderful blessings in my life.

Other thoughts of the day

_____
_____
_____
_____
_____
_____
_____
_____
_____
_____
_____
_____
_____
_____
_____
_____

The Word of the Day is:

Accomplishment

Sit quietly and relax. Now take a deep breath in through your nose and exhale slowly through your mouth. Take time to meditate on this word. What does the word mean to you? What messages do the Angels have for you regarding this word? What comes to mind? Now write it down.

Today's Date: _____

Gratitude Journal

Take a minute to think of all the things that life has given you to be thankful for.
Now I'd like you to write down ten things that you are grateful for...

1 _____
2 _____
3 _____
4 _____
5 _____
6 _____
7 _____
8 _____
9 _____
10 _____

Thank you for these wonderful blessings in my life.

Other thoughts of the day

_____
_____
_____
_____
_____
_____
_____
_____
_____
_____
_____
_____
_____
_____
_____

The Word of the Day is:

Direction

Sit quietly and relax. Now take a deep breath in through your nose and exhale slowly through your mouth. Take time to meditate on this word. What does the word mean to you? What messages do the Angels have for you regarding this word? What comes to mind? Now write it down.

Today's Date: _____

Gratitude Journal

Take a minute to think of all the things that life has given you to be thankful for.
Now I'd like you to write down ten things that you are grateful for...

1 _____
2 _____
3 _____
4 _____
5 _____
6 _____
7 _____
8 _____
9 _____
10 _____

Thank you for these wonderful blessings in my life.

Other thoughts of the day

_____
_____
_____
_____
_____
_____
_____
_____
_____
_____
_____
_____
_____
_____
_____

The Word of the Day is:

Emerging

Sit quietly and relax. Now take a deep breath in through your nose and exhale slowly through your mouth. Take time to meditate on this word. What does the word mean to you? What messages do the Angels have for you regarding this word? What comes to mind? Now write it down.

Today's Date: _____

Gratitude Journal

Take a minute to think of all the things that life has given you to be thankful for.
Now I'd like you to write down ten things that you are grateful for...

1 _____
2 _____
3 _____
4 _____
5 _____
6 _____
7 _____
8 _____
9 _____
10 _____

Thank you for these wonderful blessings in my life.

Other thoughts of the day

_____
_____
_____
_____
_____
_____
_____
_____
_____
_____
_____
_____
_____
_____
_____
_____

The Word of the Day is:

Encouragement

Sit quietly and relax. Now take a deep breath in through your nose and exhale slowly through your mouth. Take time to meditate on this word. What does the word mean to you? What messages do the Angels have for you regarding this word? What comes to mind? Now write it down.

Today's Date: _____

Gratitude Journal

Take a minute to think of all the things that life has given you to be thankful for.
Now I'd like you to write down ten things that you are grateful for...

1 _____
2 _____
3 _____
4 _____
5 _____
6 _____
7 _____
8 _____
9 _____
10 _____

Thank you for these wonderful blessings in my life.

Other thoughts of the day

_____
_____
_____
_____
_____
_____
_____
_____
_____
_____
_____
_____
_____
_____
_____

The Word of the Day is:

Friendship

Sit quietly and relax. Now take a deep breath in through your nose and exhale slowly through your mouth. Take time to meditate on this word. What does the word mean to you? What messages do the Angels have for you regarding this word? What comes to mind? Now write it down.

Today's Date: _____

Gratitude Journal

Take a minute to think of all the things that life has given you to be thankful for.
Now I'd like you to write down ten things that you are grateful for...

1 _____
2 _____
3 _____
4 _____
5 _____
6 _____
7 _____
8 _____
9 _____
10 _____

Thank you for these wonderful blessings in my life.

Other thoughts of the day

_____
_____
_____
_____
_____
_____
_____
_____
_____
_____
_____
_____
_____
_____
_____
_____

The Word of the Day is:

Powerful

Sit quietly and relax. Now take a deep breath in through your nose and exhale slowly through your mouth. Take time to meditate on this word. What does the word mean to you? What messages do the Angels have for you regarding this word? What comes to mind? Now write it down.

Today's Date: _____

Gratitude Journal

Take a minute to think of all the things that life has given you to be thankful for.
Now I'd like you to write down ten things that you are grateful for…

1 _____
2 _____
3 _____
4 _____
5 _____
6 _____
7 _____
8 _____
9 _____
10 _____

Thank you for these wonderful blessings in my life.

Other thoughts of the day

_____
_____
_____
_____
_____
_____
_____
_____
_____
_____
_____
_____
_____
_____
_____
_____

The Word of the Day is:

Honor

Sit quietly and relax. Now take a deep breath in through your nose and exhale slowly through your mouth. Take time to meditate on this word. What does the word mean to you? What messages do the Angels have for you regarding this word? What comes to mind? Now write it down.

Today's Date: _____

Gratitude Journal

Take a minute to think of all the things that life has given you to be thankful for.
Now I'd like you to write down ten things that you are grateful for...

1 _____
2 _____
3 _____
4 _____
5 _____
6 _____
7 _____
8 _____
9 _____
10 _____

Thank you for these wonderful blessings in my life.

Other thoughts of the day

_____
_____
_____
_____
_____
_____
_____
_____
_____
_____
_____
_____
_____
_____
_____

The Word of the Day is:

Surrender

Sit quietly and relax. Now take a deep breath in through your nose and exhale slowly through your mouth. Take time to meditate on this word. What does the word mean to you? What messages do the Angels have for you regarding this word? What comes to mind? Now write it down.

Today's Date: _____

Gratitude Journal

Take a minute to think of all the things that life has given you to be thankful for.
Now I'd like you to write down ten things that you are grateful for…

1 _____
2 _____
3 _____
4 _____
5 _____
6 _____
7 _____
8 _____
9 _____
10 _____

Thank you for these wonderful blessings in my life.

Other thoughts of the day

_____
_____
_____
_____
_____
_____
_____
_____
_____
_____
_____
_____
_____
_____
_____
_____

The Word of the Day is:

Appreciate

Sit quietly and relax. Now take a deep breath in through your nose and exhale slowly through your mouth. Take time to meditate on this word. What does the word mean to you? What messages do the Angels have for you regarding this word? What comes to mind? Now write it down.

Today's Date: _____

Gratitude Journal

Take a minute to think of all the things that life has given you to be thankful for.
Now I'd like you to write down ten things that you are grateful for...

1 _____
2 _____
3 _____
4 _____
5 _____
6 _____
7 _____
8 _____
9 _____
10 _____

Thank you for these wonderful blessings in my life.

Other thoughts of the day

_____
_____
_____
_____
_____
_____
_____
_____
_____
_____
_____
_____
_____
_____
_____
_____

The Word of the Day is:

Abundance

Sit quietly and relax. Now take a deep breath in through your nose and exhale slowly through your mouth. Take time to meditate on this word. What does the word mean to you? What messages do the Angels have for you regarding this word? What comes to mind? Now write it down.

Today's Date: _____

Gratitude Journal

Take a minute to think of all the things that life has given you to be thankful for.
Now I'd like you to write down ten things that you are grateful for…

1 _____
2 _____
3 _____
4 _____
5 _____
6 _____
7 _____
8 _____
9 _____
10 _____

Thank you for these wonderful blessings in my life.

Other thoughts of the day

_____
_____
_____
_____
_____
_____
_____
_____
_____
_____
_____
_____
_____
_____
_____
_____

The Word of the Day is:

Cleanse

Sit quietly and relax. Now take a deep breath in through your nose and exhale slowly through your mouth. Take time to meditate on this word. What does the word mean to you? What messages do the Angels have for you regarding this word? What comes to mind? Now write it down.

Today's Date: _____

Gratitude Journal

Take a minute to think of all the things that life has given you to be thankful for.
Now I'd like you to write down ten things that you are grateful for…

1 _____
2 _____
3 _____
4 _____
5 _____
6 _____
7 _____
8 _____
9 _____
10 _____

Thank you for these wonderful blessings in my life.

Other thoughts of the day

_____
_____
_____
_____
_____
_____
_____
_____
_____
_____
_____
_____
_____
_____
_____

The Word of the Day is:

Caring

Sit quietly and relax. Now take a deep breath in through your nose and exhale slowly through your mouth. Take time to meditate on this word. What does the word mean to you? What messages do the Angels have for you regarding this word? What comes to mind? Now write it down.

Today's Date: _____

Gratitude Journal

Take a minute to think of all the things that life has given you to be thankful for.
Now I'd like you to write down ten things that you are grateful for…

1 _____
2 _____
3 _____
4 _____
5 _____
6 _____
7 _____
8 _____
9 _____
10 _____

Thank you for these wonderful blessings in my life.

Other thoughts of the day

_____
_____
_____
_____
_____
_____
_____
_____
_____
_____
_____
_____
_____
_____
_____
_____

The Word of the Day is:

Enchantment

Sit quietly and relax. Now take a deep breath in through your nose and exhale slowly through your mouth. Take time to meditate on this word. What does the word mean to you? What messages do the Angels have for you regarding this word? What comes to mind? Now write it down.

Today's Date: _____

Gratitude Journal

Take a minute to think of all the things that life has given you to be thankful for.
Now I'd like you to write down ten things that you are grateful for...

1 _____
2 _____
3 _____
4 _____
5 _____
6 _____
7 _____
8 _____
9 _____
10 _____

Thank you for these wonderful blessings in my life.

Other thoughts of the day

_____
_____
_____
_____
_____
_____
_____
_____
_____
_____
_____
_____
_____
_____
_____
_____
_____

The Word of the Day is:

Energy

Sit quietly and relax. Now take a deep breath in through your nose and exhale slowly through your mouth. Take time to meditate on this word. What does the word mean to you? What messages do the Angels have for you regarding this word? What comes to mind? Now write it down.

Today's Date: _____

Gratitude Journal

Take a minute to think of all the things that life has given you to be thankful for.
Now I'd like you to write down ten things that you are grateful for…

1 _____
2 _____
3 _____
4 _____
5 _____
6 _____
7 _____
8 _____
9 _____
10 _____

Thank you for these wonderful blessings in my life.

Other thoughts of the day

_____
_____
_____
_____
_____
_____
_____
_____
_____
_____
_____
_____
_____
_____
_____
_____

The Word of the Day is:

Feelings

Sit quietly and relax. Now take a deep breath in through your nose and exhale slowly through your mouth. Take time to meditate on this word. What does the word mean to you? What messages do the Angels have for you regarding this word? What comes to mind? Now write it down.

Gratitude Journal

Take a minute to think of all the things that life has given you to be thankful for.
Now I'd like you to write down ten things that you are grateful for…

1 _____
2 _____
3 _____
4 _____
5 _____
6 _____
7 _____
8 _____
9 _____
10 _____

Thank you for these wonderful blessings in my life.

Other thoughts of the day

_____
_____
_____
_____
_____
_____
_____
_____
_____
_____
_____
_____
_____
_____
_____
_____

The Word of the Day is:

Imagine

Sit quietly and relax. Now take a deep breath in through your nose and exhale slowly through your mouth. Take time to meditate on this word. What does the word mean to you? What messages do the Angels have for you regarding this word? What comes to mind? Now write it down.

Today's Date: _____

Gratitude Journal

Take a minute to think of all the things that life has given you to be thankful for.
Now I'd like you to write down ten things that you are grateful for...

1 _____
2 _____
3 _____
4 _____
5 _____
6 _____
7 _____
8 _____
9 _____
10 _____

Thank you for these wonderful blessings in my life.

Other thoughts of the day

_____
_____
_____
_____
_____
_____
_____
_____
_____
_____
_____
_____
_____
_____
_____
_____

The Word of the Day is:

Kindness

Sit quietly and relax. Now take a deep breath in through your nose and exhale slowly through your mouth. Take time to meditate on this word. What does the word mean to you? What messages do the Angels have for you regarding this word? What comes to mind? Now write it down.

Today's Date: _____

Gratitude Journal

Take a minute to think of all the things that life has given you to be thankful for.
Now I'd like you to write down ten things that you are grateful for...

1 _____
2 _____
3 _____
4 _____
5 _____
6 _____
7 _____
8 _____
9 _____
10 _____

Thank you for these wonderful blessings in my life.

Other thoughts of the day

_____
_____
_____
_____
_____
_____
_____
_____
_____
_____
_____
_____
_____
_____

The Word of the Day is:

Memories

Sit quietly and relax. Now take a deep breath in through your nose and exhale slowly through your mouth. Take time to meditate on this word. What does the word mean to you? What messages do the Angels have for you regarding this word? What comes to mind? Now write it down.

Today's Date: _____

Gratitude Journal

Take a minute to think of all the things that life has given you to be thankful for.
Now I'd like you to write down ten things that you are grateful for...

1 _____
2 _____
3 _____
4 _____
5 _____
6 _____
7 _____
8 _____
9 _____
10 _____

Thank you for these wonderful blessings in my life.

Other thoughts of the day

_____
_____
_____
_____
_____
_____
_____
_____
_____
_____
_____
_____
_____
_____
_____
_____
_____

The Word of the Day is:

Meditate

Sit quietly and relax. Now take a deep breath in through your nose and exhale slowly through your mouth. Take time to meditate on this word. What does the word mean to you? What messages do the Angels have for you regarding this word? What comes to mind? Now write it down.

Today's Date: _____

Gratitude Journal

Take a minute to think of all the things that life has given you to be thankful for.
Now I'd like you to write down ten things that you are grateful for...

1 _____
2 _____
3 _____
4 _____
5 _____
6 _____
7 _____
8 _____
9 _____
10 _____

Thank you for these wonderful blessings in my life.

Other thoughts of the day

_____
_____
_____
_____
_____
_____
_____
_____
_____
_____
_____
_____
_____
_____
_____

The Word of the Day is:

Crystals

Sit quietly and relax. Now take a deep breath in through your nose and exhale slowly through your mouth. Take time to meditate on this word. What does the word mean to you? What messages do the Angels have for you regarding this word? What comes to mind? Now write it down.

Today's Date: _____

Gratitude Journal

Take a minute to think of all the things that life has given you to be thankful for.
Now I'd like you to write down ten things that you are grateful for...

1 _____
2 _____
3 _____
4 _____
5 _____
6 _____
7 _____
8 _____
9 _____
10 _____

Thank you for these wonderful blessings in my life.

Other thoughts of the day

_____
_____
_____
_____
_____
_____
_____
_____
_____
_____
_____
_____
_____
_____
_____

The Word of the Day is:

Wind

Sit quietly and relax. Now take a deep breath in through your nose and exhale slowly through your mouth. Take time to meditate on this word. What does the word mean to you? What messages do the Angels have for you regarding this word? What comes to mind? Now write it down.

Today's Date: _____

Gratitude Journal

Take a minute to think of all the things that life has given you to be thankful for.
Now I'd like you to write down ten things that you are grateful for...

1 _____
2 _____
3 _____
4 _____
5 _____
6 _____
7 _____
8 _____
9 _____
10 _____

Thank you for these wonderful blessings in my life.

Other thoughts of the day

_____
_____
_____
_____
_____
_____
_____
_____
_____
_____
_____
_____
_____
_____
_____

The Word of the Day is:

Heaven

Sit quietly and relax. Now take a deep breath in through your nose and exhale slowly through your mouth. Take time to meditate on this word. What does the word mean to you? What messages do the Angels have for you regarding this word? What comes to mind? Now write it down.

Today's Date: _____

Gratitude Journal

Take a minute to think of all the things that life has given you to be thankful for.
Now I'd like you to write down ten things that you are grateful for…

1 _____
2 _____
3 _____
4 _____
5 _____
6 _____
7 _____
8 _____
9 _____
10 _____

Thank you for these wonderful blessings in my life.

Other thoughts of the day

_____
_____
_____
_____
_____
_____
_____
_____
_____
_____
_____
_____
_____
_____
_____
_____

The Word of the Day is:

Angels

Sit quietly and relax. Now take a deep breath in through your nose and exhale slowly through your mouth. Take time to meditate on this word. What does the word mean to you? What messages do the Angels have for you regarding this word? What comes to mind? Now write it down.

Today's Date: _____

Gratitude Journal

Take a minute to think of all the things that life has given you to be thankful for.
Now I'd like you to write down ten things that you are grateful for...

1 _____
2 _____
3 _____
4 _____
5 _____
6 _____
7 _____
8 _____
9 _____
10 _____

Thank you for these wonderful blessings in my life.

Other thoughts of the day

_____
_____
_____
_____
_____
_____
_____
_____
_____
_____
_____
_____
_____
_____
_____
_____

The Word of the Day is:

Romance

Sit quietly and relax. Now take a deep breath in through your nose and exhale slowly through your mouth. Take time to meditate on this word. What does the word mean to you? What messages do the Angels have for you regarding this word? What comes to mind? Now write it down.

Today's Date: _____

Gratitude Journal

Take a minute to think of all the things that life has given you to be thankful for.
Now I'd like you to write down ten things that you are grateful for...

1 _____
2 _____
3 _____
4 _____
5 _____
6 _____
7 _____
8 _____
9 _____
10 _____

Thank you for these wonderful blessings in my life.

Other thoughts of the day

_____
_____
_____
_____
_____
_____
_____
_____
_____
_____
_____
_____
_____
_____
_____

The Word of the Day is:

Soul-mate

Sit quietly and relax. Now take a deep breath in through your nose and exhale slowly through your mouth. Take time to meditate on this word. What does the word mean to you? What messages do the Angels have for you regarding this word? What comes to mind? Now write it down.

Today's Date: _____

Gratitude Journal

Take a minute to think of all the things that life has given you to be thankful for.
Now I'd like you to write down ten things that you are grateful for...

1 _____
2 _____
3 _____
4 _____
5 _____
6 _____
7 _____
8 _____
9 _____
10 _____

Thank you for these wonderful blessings in my life.

Other thoughts of the day

_____
_____
_____
_____
_____
_____
_____
_____
_____
_____
_____
_____
_____
_____

The Word of the Day is:

Affirmations

Sit quietly and relax. Now take a deep breath in through your nose and exhale slowly through your mouth. Take time to meditate on this word. What does the word mean to you? What messages do the Angels have for you regarding this word? What comes to mind? Now write it down.

Today's Date: _____

Gratitude Journal

Take a minute to think of all the things that life has given you to be thankful for.
Now I'd like you to write down ten things that you are grateful for...

1 _____
2 _____
3 _____
4 _____
5 _____
6 _____
7 _____
8 _____
9 _____
10 _____

Thank you for these wonderful blessings in my life.

Other thoughts of the day

_____
_____
_____
_____
_____
_____
_____
_____
_____
_____
_____
_____
_____
_____
_____

The Word of the Day is:

Sunrise

Sit quietly and relax. Now take a deep breath in through your nose and exhale slowly through your mouth. Take time to meditate on this word. What does the word mean to you? What messages do the Angels have for you regarding this word? What comes to mind? Now write it down.

Today's Date: _____

Gratitude Journal

Take a minute to think of all the things that life has given you to be thankful for.
Now I'd like you to write down ten things that you are grateful for...

1 _____
2 _____
3 _____
4 _____
5 _____
6 _____
7 _____
8 _____
9 _____
10 _____

Thank you for these wonderful blessings in my life.

Other thoughts of the day

_____
_____
_____
_____
_____
_____
_____
_____
_____
_____
_____
_____
_____
_____
_____
_____

The Word of the Day is:

Peace

Sit quietly and relax. Now take a deep breath in through your nose and exhale slowly through your mouth. Take time to meditate on this word. What does the word mean to you? What messages do the Angels have for you regarding this word? What comes to mind? Now write it down.

Today's Date: _____

Gratitude Journal

Take a minute to think of all the things that life has given you to be thankful for.
Now I'd like you to write down ten things that you are grateful for...

1 _____
2 _____
3 _____
4 _____
5 _____
6 _____
7 _____
8 _____
9 _____
10 _____

Thank you for these wonderful blessings in my life.

Other thoughts of the day

_____
_____
_____
_____
_____
_____
_____
_____
_____
_____
_____
_____
_____
_____

The Word of the Day is:

Transformation

Sit quietly and relax. Now take a deep breath in through your nose and exhale slowly through your mouth. Take time to meditate on this word. What does the word mean to you? What messages do the Angels have for you regarding this word? What comes to mind? Now write it down.

Today's Date: _____

Gratitude Journal

Take a minute to think of all the things that life has given you to be thankful for.
Now I'd like you to write down ten things that you are grateful for...

1 _____
2 _____
3 _____
4 _____
5 _____
6 _____
7 _____
8 _____
9 _____
10 _____

Thank you for these wonderful blessings in my life.

Other thoughts of the day

_____
_____
_____
_____
_____
_____
_____
_____
_____
_____
_____
_____
_____
_____
_____

The Word of the Day is:

Remembrance

Sit quietly and relax. Now take a deep breath in through your nose and exhale slowly through your mouth. Take time to meditate on this word. What does the word mean to you? What messages do the Angels have for you regarding this word? What comes to mind? Now write it down.

Today's Date: _____

Gratitude Journal

Take a minute to think of all the things that life has given you to be thankful for.
Now I'd like you to write down ten things that you are grateful for...

1 _____
2 _____
3 _____
4 _____
5 _____
6 _____
7 _____
8 _____
9 _____
10 _____

Thank you for these wonderful blessings in my life.

Other thoughts of the day

_____
_____
_____
_____
_____
_____
_____
_____
_____
_____
_____
_____
_____
_____
_____
_____

The Word of the Day is:

Helpful

Sit quietly and relax. Now take a deep breath in through your nose and exhale slowly through your mouth. Take time to meditate on this word. What does the word mean to you? What messages do the Angels have for you regarding this word? What comes to mind? Now write it down.

Today's Date: _____

Gratitude Journal

Take a minute to think of all the things that life has given you to be thankful for.
Now I'd like you to write down ten things that you are grateful for…

1 _____
2 _____
3 _____
4 _____
5 _____
6 _____
7 _____
8 _____
9 _____
10 _____

Thank you for these wonderful blessings in my life.

Other thoughts of the day

_____
_____
_____
_____
_____
_____
_____
_____
_____
_____
_____
_____
_____
_____
_____

The Word of the Day is:

Freedom

Sit quietly and relax. Now take a deep breath in through your nose and exhale slowly through your mouth. Take time to meditate on this word. What does the word mean to you? What messages do the Angels have for you regarding this word? What comes to mind? Now write it down.

Today's Date: _____

Gratitude Journal

Take a minute to think of all the things that life has given you to be thankful for.
Now I'd like you to write down ten things that you are grateful for...

1 _____
2 _____
3 _____
4 _____
5 _____
6 _____
7 _____
8 _____
9 _____
10 _____

Thank you for these wonderful blessings in my life.

Other thoughts of the day

_____
_____
_____
_____
_____
_____
_____
_____
_____
_____
_____
_____
_____
_____
_____

The Word of the Day is:

Optimistic

Sit quietly and relax. Now take a deep breath in through your nose and exhale slowly through your mouth. Take time to meditate on this word. What does the word mean to you? What messages do the Angels have for you regarding this word? What comes to mind? Now write it down.

Today's Date: _____

Gratitude Journal

Take a minute to think of all the things that life has given you to be thankful for.
Now I'd like you to write down ten things that you are grateful for…

1 _____
2 _____
3 _____
4 _____
5 _____
6 _____
7 _____
8 _____
9 _____
10 _____

Thank you for these wonderful blessings in my life.

Other thoughts of the day

_____
_____
_____
_____
_____
_____
_____
_____
_____
_____
_____
_____
_____
_____
_____

The Word of the Day is:

Respectful

Sit quietly and relax. Now take a deep breath in through your nose and exhale slowly through your mouth. Take time to meditate on this word. What does the word mean to you? What messages do the Angels have for you regarding this word? What comes to mind? Now write it down.

Today's Date: _____

Gratitude Journal

Take a minute to think of all the things that life has given you to be thankful for.
Now I'd like you to write down ten things that you are grateful for...

1 _____
2 _____
3 _____
4 _____
5 _____
6 _____
7 _____
8 _____
9 _____
10 _____

Thank you for these wonderful blessings in my life.

Other thoughts of the day

_____
_____
_____
_____
_____
_____
_____
_____
_____
_____
_____
_____
_____
_____

The Word of the Day is:

Challenge

Sit quietly and relax. Now take a deep breath in through your nose and exhale slowly through your mouth. Take time to meditate on this word. What does the word mean to you? What messages do the Angels have for you regarding this word? What comes to mind? Now write it down.

Today's Date: _____

Gratitude Journal

Take a minute to think of all the things that life has given you to be thankful for.
Now I'd like you to write down ten things that you are grateful for...

1 _____
2 _____
3 _____
4 _____
5 _____
6 _____
7 _____
8 _____
9 _____
10 _____

Thank you for these wonderful blessings in my life.

Other thoughts of the day

_____
_____
_____
_____
_____
_____
_____
_____
_____
_____
_____
_____
_____
_____
_____
_____

The Word of the Day is:

Revelation

Sit quietly and relax. Now take a deep breath in through your nose and exhale slowly through your mouth. Take time to meditate on this word. What does the word mean to you? What messages do the Angels have for you regarding this word? What comes to mind? Now write it down.

Today's Date: _____

Gratitude Journal

Take a minute to think of all the things that life has given you to be thankful for.
Now I'd like you to write down ten things that you are grateful for...

1 _____
2 _____
3 _____
4 _____
5 _____
6 _____
7 _____
8 _____
9 _____
10 _____

Thank you for these wonderful blessings in my life.

Other thoughts of the day

_____
_____
_____
_____
_____
_____
_____
_____
_____
_____
_____
_____
_____
_____
_____
_____
_____

The Word of the Day is:

Sit quietly and relax. Now take a deep breath in through your nose and exhale slowly through your mouth. Take time to meditate on this word. What does the word mean to you? What messages do the Angels have for you regarding this word? What comes to mind? Now write it down.

Today's Date: _____

Gratitude Journal

Take a minute to think of all the things that life has given you to be thankful for.
Now I'd like you to write down ten things that you are grateful for…

1 _____
2 _____
3 _____
4 _____
5 _____
6 _____
7 _____
8 _____
9 _____
10 _____

Thank you for these wonderful blessings in my life.

Other thoughts of the day

_____
_____
_____
_____
_____
_____
_____
_____
_____
_____
_____
_____
_____
_____

The Word of the Day is:

Dedication

Sit quietly and relax. Now take a deep breath in through your nose and exhale slowly through your mouth. Take time to meditate on this word. What does the word mean to you? What messages do the Angels have for you regarding this word? What comes to mind? Now write it down.

Today's Date: _____

Gratitude Journal

Take a minute to think of all the things that life has given you to be thankful for.
Now I'd like you to write down ten things that you are grateful for...

1 _____
2 _____
3 _____
4 _____
5 _____
6 _____
7 _____
8 _____
9 _____
10 _____

Thank you for these wonderful blessings in my life.

Other thoughts of the day

_____
_____
_____
_____
_____
_____
_____
_____
_____
_____
_____
_____
_____
_____
_____
_____

The Word of the Day is:

Timing

Sit quietly and relax. Now take a deep breath in through your nose and exhale slowly through your mouth. Take time to meditate on this word. What does the word mean to you? What messages do the Angels have for you regarding this word? What comes to mind? Now write it down.

Today's Date: _____

Gratitude Journal

Take a minute to think of all the things that life has given you to be thankful for.
Now I'd like you to write down ten things that you are grateful for…

1 _____
2 _____
3 _____
4 _____
5 _____
6 _____
7 _____
8 _____
9 _____
10 _____

Thank you for these wonderful blessings in my life.

Other thoughts of the day

_____
_____
_____
_____
_____
_____
_____
_____
_____
_____
_____
_____
_____
_____
_____
_____

The Word of the Day is:

Divinity

Sit quietly and relax. Now take a deep breath in through your nose and exhale slowly through your mouth. Take time to meditate on this word. What does the word mean to you? What messages do the Angels have for you regarding this word? What comes to mind? Now write it down.

Today's Date: _____

Gratitude Journal

Take a minute to think of all the things that life has given you to be thankful for.
Now I'd like you to write down ten things that you are grateful for...

1 _____
2 _____
3 _____
4 _____
5 _____
6 _____
7 _____
8 _____
9 _____
10 _____

Thank you for these wonderful blessings in my life.

Other thoughts of the day

_____
_____
_____
_____
_____
_____
_____
_____
_____
_____
_____
_____
_____
_____
_____

The Word of the Day is:

Beautiful

Sit quietly and relax. Now take a deep breath in through your nose and exhale slowly through your mouth. Take time to meditate on this word. What does the word mean to you? What messages do the Angels have for you regarding this word? What comes to mind? Now write it down.

Today's Date: _____

Gratitude Journal

Take a minute to think of all the things that life has given you to be thankful for.
Now I'd like you to write down ten things that you are grateful for...

1 _____
2 _____
3 _____
4 _____
5 _____
6 _____
7 _____
8 _____
9 _____
10 _____

Thank you for these wonderful blessings in my life.

Other thoughts of the day

_____
_____
_____
_____
_____
_____
_____
_____
_____
_____
_____
_____
_____
_____

The Word of the Day is:

Innocence

Sit quietly and relax. Now take a deep breath in through your nose and exhale slowly through your mouth. Take time to meditate on this word. What does the word mean to you? What messages do the Angels have for you regarding this word? What comes to mind? Now write it down.

Today's Date: _____

Gratitude Journal

Take a minute to think of all the things that life has given you to be thankful for.
Now I'd like you to write down ten things that you are grateful for...

1 _____
2 _____
3 _____
4 _____
5 _____
6 _____
7 _____
8 _____
9 _____
10 _____

Thank you for these wonderful blessings in my life.

Other thoughts of the day

_____
_____
_____
_____
_____
_____
_____
_____
_____
_____
_____
_____
_____
_____
_____
_____

The Word of the Day is:

Wish

Sit quietly and relax. Now take a deep breath in through your nose and exhale slowly through your mouth. Take time to meditate on this word. What does the word mean to you? What messages do the Angels have for you regarding this word? What comes to mind? Now write it down.

Today's Date: _____

Gratitude Journal

Take a minute to think of all the things that life has given you to be thankful for.
Now I'd like you to write down ten things that you are grateful for...

1 _____
2 _____
3 _____
4 _____
5 _____
6 _____
7 _____
8 _____
9 _____
10 _____

Thank you for these wonderful blessings in my life.

Other thoughts of the day

_____
_____
_____
_____
_____
_____
_____
_____
_____
_____
_____
_____
_____
_____
_____

The Word of the Day is:

Fulfillment

Sit quietly and relax. Now take a deep breath in through your nose and exhale slowly through your mouth. Take time to meditate on this word. What does the word mean to you? What messages do the Angels have for you regarding this word? What comes to mind? Now write it down.

Today's Date: _____

Gratitude Journal

Take a minute to think of all the things that life has given you to be thankful for.
Now I'd like you to write down ten things that you are grateful for…

1 _____
2 _____
3 _____
4 _____
5 _____
6 _____
7 _____
8 _____
9 _____
10 _____

Thank you for these wonderful blessings in my life.

Other thoughts of the day

_____
_____
_____
_____
_____
_____
_____
_____
_____
_____
_____
_____
_____
_____
_____
_____
_____

The Word of the Day is:

Protection

❦

Sit quietly and relax. Now take a deep breath in through your nose and exhale slowly through your mouth. Take time to meditate on this word. What does the word mean to you? What messages do the Angels have for you regarding this word? What comes to mind? Now write it down.

Today's Date: _____

Gratitude Journal

Take a minute to think of all the things that life has given you to be thankful for.
Now I'd like you to write down ten things that you are grateful for...

1 _____
2 _____
3 _____
4 _____
5 _____
6 _____
7 _____
8 _____
9 _____
10 _____

Thank you for these wonderful blessings in my life.

Other thoughts of the day

_____
_____
_____
_____
_____
_____
_____
_____
_____
_____
_____
_____
_____
_____

The Word of the Day is:

Spirit

Sit quietly and relax. Now take a deep breath in through your nose and exhale slowly through your mouth. Take time to meditate on this word. What does the word mean to you? What messages do the Angels have for you regarding this word? What comes to mind? Now write it down.

Today's Date: _____

Gratitude Journal

Take a minute to think of all the things that life has given you to be thankful for.
Now I'd like you to write down ten things that you are grateful for...

1 _____
2 _____
3 _____
4 _____
5 _____
6 _____
7 _____
8 _____
9 _____
10 _____

Thank you for these wonderful blessings in my life.

Other thoughts of the day

_____
_____
_____
_____
_____
_____
_____
_____
_____
_____
_____
_____
_____
_____
_____

The Word of the Day is:

Healing

Sit quietly and relax. Now take a deep breath in through your nose and exhale slowly through your mouth. Take time to meditate on this word. What does the word mean to you? What messages do the Angels have for you regarding this word? What comes to mind? Now write it down.

Today's Date: _____

Gratitude Journal

Take a minute to think of all the things that life has given you to be thankful for.
Now I'd like you to write down ten things that you are grateful for…

1 _____
2 _____
3 _____
4 _____
5 _____
6 _____
7 _____
8 _____
9 _____
10 _____

Thank you for these wonderful blessings in my life.

Other thoughts of the day

_____
_____
_____
_____
_____
_____
_____
_____
_____
_____
_____
_____
_____
_____
_____
_____

The Word of the Day is:

Destiny

Sit quietly and relax. Now take a deep breath in through your nose and exhale slowly through your mouth. Take time to meditate on this word. What does the word mean to you? What messages do the Angels have for you regarding this word? What comes to mind? Now write it down.

Today's Date: _____

Gratitude Journal

Take a minute to think of all the things that life has given you to be thankful for.
Now I'd like you to write down ten things that you are grateful for...

1 _____
2 _____
3 _____
4 _____
5 _____
6 _____
7 _____
8 _____
9 _____
10 _____

Thank you for these wonderful blessings in my life.

Other thoughts of the day

_____
_____
_____
_____
_____
_____
_____
_____
_____
_____
_____
_____
_____
_____
_____
_____

The Word of the Day is:

Decisions

Sit quietly and relax. Now take a deep breath in through your nose and exhale slowly through your mouth. Take time to meditate on this word. What does the word mean to you? What messages do the Angels have for you regarding this word? What comes to mind? Now write it down.

Today's Date: _____

Gratitude Journal

Take a minute to think of all the things that life has given you to be thankful for.
Now I'd like you to write down ten things that you are grateful for...

1 _____
2 _____
3 _____
4 _____
5 _____
6 _____
7 _____
8 _____
9 _____
10 _____

Thank you for these wonderful blessings in my life.

Other thoughts of the day

_____
_____
_____
_____
_____
_____
_____
_____
_____
_____
_____
_____
_____
_____
_____
_____

The Word of the Day is:

Journey

Sit quietly and relax. Now take a deep breath in through your nose and exhale slowly through your mouth. Take time to meditate on this word. What does the word mean to you? What messages do the Angels have for you regarding this word? What comes to mind? Now write it down.

Today's Date: _____

Gratitude Journal

Take a minute to think of all the things that life has given you to be thankful for.
Now I'd like you to write down ten things that you are grateful for...

1 _____
2 _____
3 _____
4 _____
5 _____
6 _____
7 _____
8 _____
9 _____
10 _____

Thank you for these wonderful blessings in my life.

Other thoughts of the day

_____
_____
_____
_____
_____
_____
_____
_____
_____
_____
_____
_____
_____
_____
_____
_____

The Word of the Day is:

Twin-Flame

Sit quietly and relax. Now take a deep breath in through your nose and exhale slowly through your mouth. Take time to meditate on this word. What does the word mean to you? What messages do the Angels have for you regarding this word? What comes to mind? Now write it down.

Today's Date: _____

Gratitude Journal

Take a minute to think of all the things that life has given you to be thankful for.
Now I'd like you to write down ten things that you are grateful for...

1 _____
2 _____
3 _____
4 _____
5 _____
6 _____
7 _____
8 _____
9 _____
10 _____

Thank you for these wonderful blessings in my life.

Other thoughts of the day

_____
_____
_____
_____
_____
_____
_____
_____
_____
_____
_____
_____
_____
_____
_____

The Word of the Day is:

Mission

Sit quietly and relax. Now take a deep breath in through your nose and exhale slowly through your mouth. Take time to meditate on this word. What does the word mean to you? What messages do the Angels have for you regarding this word? What comes to mind? Now write it down.

Today's Date: _____

Gratitude Journal

Take a minute to think of all the things that life has given you to be thankful for.
Now I'd like you to write down ten things that you are grateful for...

1 _____
2 _____
3 _____
4 _____
5 _____
6 _____
7 _____
8 _____
9 _____
10 _____

Thank you for these wonderful blessings in my life.

Other thoughts of the day

_____
_____
_____
_____
_____
_____
_____
_____
_____
_____
_____
_____
_____
_____
_____

The Word of the Day is:

Purpose

Sit quietly and relax. Now take a deep breath in through your nose and exhale slowly through your mouth. Take time to meditate on this word. What does the word mean to you? What messages do the Angels have for you regarding this word? What comes to mind? Now write it down.

Today's Date: _____

Gratitude Journal

Take a minute to think of all the things that life has given you to be thankful for.
Now I'd like you to write down ten things that you are grateful for...

1 _____
2 _____
3 _____
4 _____
5 _____
6 _____
7 _____
8 _____
9 _____
10 _____

Thank you for these wonderful blessings in my life.

Other thoughts of the day

_____
_____
_____
_____
_____
_____
_____
_____
_____
_____
_____
_____
_____
_____
_____
_____